/lH Publishing Limited
on
  6 5 4 3 2 1
sed
  6 5 4 3 2
sed
  6 5 4

by: L. Mike Henry / K. Sean Harris
ign: Susan Lee-Quee
· Clovis Brown
Typesetting: Michelle M. Mitchell

by: LMH Publishing Limited
 Road,
trial Complex
 0
 C.S.O., Jamaica
38-0005; 938-0712
759-8752
hbookpublishing@cwjamaica.com

China   ISBN: 978-976-8184-29-0

LMH Official Dicti

Popula
JAMAIC
Phras

Compiled by
L. Mike Henry / K. Sea

© 2002
First Ed
10 9 8
2003 Re
10 9 8
2006 Re
10 9 8

All rigl
or trar
recordi

The pu
inadve
the firs

If you
propei
book,

All LI
bulk p

Comp
Cove
Illust
Desi

Pub
7 No
LOJ
Buil
Kin
Tel:
Fax
Ema

Pri

Publisher's Notes

LMH Publishing is pleased to produce the first eleven books in a series of titles which will treat the Jamaican culture in a serious yet entertaining format.

The first eleven titles in this series are:
- LMH Official Dictionary of Jamaican Words & Proverbs
- LMH Official Dictionary of Popular Jamaican Phrases
- LMH Official Dictionary of Jamaican History
- LMH Official Dictionary of Jamaican Herbs & Medicinal Plants and their uses.
- LMH Official Dictionary of Caribbean Herbs & Medicinal Plants and their uses.
- LMH Official Dictionary of Sex Island Style
- LMH Official Dictionary of Sex Island Style Vol. 2
- LMH Official Dictionary of Caribbean Exotic Fruits
- LMH Official Dictionary of Jamaican Religious Practices & Revival Cults
- LMH Official Dictionary of Bahamian Words & Proverbs
- LMH Official Dictionary of Popular Bahamian Phrases

As this series cannot be complete without the response of our readers (as no other publisher has yet attempted to record our culture) we implore you, our readers, to voice your opinions, comments and observations which we will take into consideration when publishing new editions.

I hope you enjoy our witty and innovative series. See you next time.

Mike Henry
Publisher

LMH Official Dictionary of

Popular
JAMAICAN
Phrases

"A go Foreign"

A go foreign. (illus.)

To travel to another country. "Mi a go foreign nex week!" I'm going overseas next week. Being able to travel to other countries is a big thing for most Jamaicans and they are somewhat envied by those who for various reasons are not able to travel.

A it dis.

This is it. One might take a cab and when your destination is reached, the driver may say "A it dis." This is it, you've arrived.

A so yuh gwaan.

So thats how you're going to act. You might be appalled or disappointed by someone's actions and you say to them "A so yuh gwaan!"

A it mek.

That is the cause or reason. "A it mek she always so sick." That is the reason she's always so sick.

3

A idiat t'ing dat.

That is foolishness. When one sees or hears of anything that does not make sense, one might comment "A idiat t'ing dat!"

A wha do yuh.

What is wrong with you. May be used in concern as well as in annoyance. For instance if someone is bothering you, you might shout "A wha do yuh man!" What the hell is wrong with you!

A wha dis fadda?

What is this father? In this instance father refers to God. So in using this phrase one is asking God what is this I see, or what is this that's happening to me.

All fruits ripe.

Everything is going great. Phrase made popular by a hit song from a local singer.

Bawn back a cow.

You tell someone that they "bawn back a cow," you're telling them that they are stupid. Mostly heard in the rural areas.

Bearin' wheel skate.

A scooter made from scrap lumber and bearings. Being poor does not stop the average Jamaican kid from having toys, he'll make them himself!

Belly a front, belly a back.

Someone who possesses "belly a front, belly a back," has a paunch and a large rump.

Bench an' batty. (illus.)

Refers to two people who are inseparable or always seen together. "Paul an' Gary a like bench an batty." Paul and Gary are inseparable.

"Bench 'n Batty"

Ben Johnson day.

The day before payday, usually a Thursday.

Blouse an' skirt.

An exclamation used when one is surprised or amazed by something. Someone might see an amazing stunt while viewing a movie and exclaim "blouse an' skirt!"

Bob an' weave.

To avoid someone or to run around in circles.

Book of laws.

No, it does not refer to the Bible. It's simply the local term for cow intestines.

Buzz Mi Likkle More.

Call me later.

Clamp dung.

To "clamp dung" is to control or prohibit.

Clear off bwoy!

Get away from here boy!

Coco maca tick.

A stick made from pimento wood and is a yard in length. It is believed to have a duppy (ghost) captured in it. It is used in the practice of obeah.(voodoo)

Caa get tru.

"Mi caa get tru!" I cannot get through or I'm not succeeding.

Dash weh belly.

To "dash weh belly" is to have an abortion. Jamaican girls who "dash weh bellies" are looked upon with contempt by their male counter-parts.

Dash mi weh.

If someone says to you "Yuh dash mi weh," that means you have forgotten about them. Usually said if you haven't gone to see someone whom you usually visit in a long time.

8

Deh ya so.

Here. "De coat deh ya so." The coat is here.

Dinki minie.

A type of dance that is done at a wake.

Dip an fall back.

A fondue made from coconut milk and salt fish. Jamaican delicacy.

Doah come strait.

Someone who "doah come strait" is a crooked and deceitful person.

Donkey years.

If you haven't seen someone in "donkey years", you haven't seen them in a very long time.

Draw bad caad.

To suffer great misfortune or to experience bad luck.

"Draw bad caad"

Dry lan' touris'.

A very boastful person who acts as though he's a visitor to the island.

Eh go so.

That's the way it goes. Someone asks you if something is true and you reply "Eh go so", it's true.

Fallah fashin.

To copy or imitate the actions of others.

Finga dem lite.

If people don't want you to visit their homes because "yuh finga dem lite", it's because you love to steal. Simply put, you're a thief.

Force ripe.

Anything that has ripened prematurely, including young girls who act like grown women.

Free paypa bun.

To lose one's freedom. Usually said when holidays are over and the children have to go to school or if your vacation has come to an end and you have to go back to work.

Full a mout'.

Someone who is "full a mout'" is all talk and no action.

Full 'undred.

To give the whole information or tell everything. "Gi mi de full 'undred bout wha 'appen laas nite." Tell me everything that happened last night.

Fyah bun.

An expression used when denouncing someone or something. For instance one might say "Fyah bun fi rapis!" Denouncing all rapists.

Gwaan like yuh nice.

To "gwaan like yuh nice" is to act above your station. Pretending to be of the upper class when one is not. Usually used in reference to women who act snobbish.

Gaan to bed.

A whole lot. "Mi love mi wife gaan to bed!" I love my wife a lot.

Gettin aan.

Coping. "'Ow she getting aan?" How is she coping?

Gi yuh bun.

If your significant other "a gi yuh bun", he or she is cheating on you.

Gi mi six fi nine. (illus.)

To be lied to, fooled or tricked.

"Gi mi six fi a nine"

Gi mi weh.

To be given up for adoption.

Gi a bly.

To show courtesy on the road to other drivers.

Goal teet', don gorgon.

Such an individual is recognized as a don or big shot.

Hear dis.

When one says "Hear dis!" he's emphasizing that you need to listen.

Heng pon mi.

A cloth sack worn around the neck, used to hold things — sort of like a pocket.

Head a tek wata.

If your "head a tek wata", you should be concerned because that means you are going crazy.

Head pawt stunted.

Used to describe someone who is retarded or just stupid.

Heggs up.

To get ahead of yourself.

Hell an' powda 'ouse.

A serious confrontation. "A hell an' powda 'ouse if mi nuh get mi money!" There will be a serious confrontation if I don't get my money.

Heng pon nail.

Untidy; Dishevelled. "Yuh fava heng pon nail." You look very untidy.

Hile a ride mi.

The state of being extremely horny.

Hush yuh mout'.

Be quiet.

Jackass rope.

Tobacco twisted into rope form.

Jah rastafari.

Praise God! A chant said by Rastafarians.

Jing bang.

Undesirables. One's mother might yell at him "Tap heng out wid jing bang befo yuh get inna trouble." Stop hanging out with bad company before you get in trouble.

Jook out.

To prick or stick someone or something. "Mine yuh jook out mi yeye!" Be careful, you almost poked me in the eye.

Jump alleluia.

To jump and dance in a celebratory manner, usually in a church or at a revival.

Jus lef mi.

Just leave me alone.

Ketch yuh back.

To catch up with you.

Kibba yuh mout'.

Shut your mouth.

Kin teet'.

Wide grins that show most of your teeth. "Yuh nuh tap kin yuh teet'." You haven't stopped grinning.

Kiss mi neck.

An expression of surprise. If someone that you least expected came to visit you, you might exclaim "Kiss mi neck!"

Kiss teet'.

Hissing sound made by drawing air through the teeth. Considered to be a rude and disrespectful act. Kids who "kiss teet'" in the presence of adults are immediately reprimanded.

Knock up.

To get pregnant.

Laas caa fine.

It's lost and cannot be found.

Labba labba.

One who is "labba labba" talks too much.

Lawd a massy.

Lord have mercy, an exclamation.

Lay wait.

An ambush or to wait on somebody.

Leggo de bwoy.

Advice given to females whose spouse is not treating them right. Leave him alone!

Ley ley.

To "ley ley" means to waste time. Can also mean to relax. "Mi deh yah a ley ley." I'm here relaxing.

19

Lib well.

To lead an affluent lifestyle. Living well.

Lik fi six.

To do well.

Lik-pot-sweet finga.

Your index finger.

Like yuh madda.

Like your mother. Terms like this will most certainly have you brawling if uttered to the wrong person.

Link Mi Pon Di Cellie.

Call me on my cell phone.

Long out.

To protrude or stick out. "Long out yuh han'." Extend your hand.

Macca fat.

A tough gummy fruit the size of a ping pong ball.

Main squeeze. (illus.)

Your significant other.

Man a shatta.

Someone who proclaims "Man a shatta", is saying that he's a respected guy on the street.

Mannish wata.

A soup made with a goat's head reputed to increase a man's virility. What is a fact though, is that drinking this after consuming too much alcohol will sober you up.

Mash up.

Broken beyond repair. Also refers to one who used to be affluent but has now fallen on hard times.

"main squeeze"

Massa God.

My God. "Massa God nah let mi dung."
God will not let me down.

Mek four yeye.

To get together.

Mi an' yuh deh.

You and I are romantically involved.

Mi nah experience it.

That won't be happening to me.
Learning from someone else's
experience.

Mi nuh know.

I don't know.

Mi raas!

An extremely popular but profane
exclamation.

Mo fyah!

An expression of excitement.
"Mo fyah!" meaning more hotness.

Mout'-a-massy.

A woman who is constantly gossiping.

Murda a soun' bwoy.

No, it does not mean to literally kill somebody. It's a term used when disc jockeys compete against each other musically.

Mus mus.

A mouse.

Naa man.

An emphatic no! When you ask someone to do you a favour, and they reply "Naa man!" Forget about it.

Name bran'.

Anything material such as a car or clothes that is by a popular designer is considered to be "name bran'".

Nasty nayga.

A derogatory term used to describe people who you feel are below your level.

Natty dread.

Another term for dreadlocks or Rastafanrians.

Neegle yeye pum-pum.

Vagina that is considered tight. Hence the analogy to the needle's eye.

Nex' time.

Next time.

Nice nuh raas.

Extremely enjoyable. "De club nice nuh raas!" The club is very nice. Rather profane though.

Nice fi jook.

When a female is "nice fi jook". She's fantastic in bed.

Nine nite.

A wake which is held on the ninth night after someone dies. Usually crowded especially in the rural areas. Lots of eating, drinking and singing.

Nose naat.

Snot from the nostrils.

Nuff nuff.

An abundance. You ask someone how much money he has and he replies "Nuff nuff!" he has a lot.

Nuff respect.

When you have "nuff respect" for a person, you have the utmost respect for them.

Nuh badda wid dat.

Don't bother with that. Someone might tell you that they're about to do something stupid and you say. "Nuh badda wid dat."

Nuh 'kin teet.

Don't laugh or be too friendly.

Nuh lie.

Pleading with someone to tell you the truth.

Nuh lotion, pet nor powda.

No pampering. "Mi nah lotion, pet nor powda nuh gal!" I'm not pampering any girl, a local tough guy might proclaim.

Nuh tek tea.

Not compatible. "Mi an im nuh tek tea." He and I do not get along.

Nuh watch nutten.

Don't worry about a thing.

Nyam an gu weh.

One who eats and leaves as he is finished.

Nyam too much. (illus.)
Eats too much.

Obeah man.
One who practices voodoo or black magic.

One one.
Singly, slowly; separately. A popular saying is "One, one coco full basket."

Ouse top.
The roof of a house.

Out fi.
About to. "Mi out fi gwaan a de pawty." I'm about to go to the party.

Outa auda.
Out of order. Also rude or disrespectful. "De likkle bwoy outa auda yuh see!" The little boy is so rude!

"nyam too much"

Passa passa.

"Mi nuh inna nuh passa passa wid oonu!" I am not getting involved in any controversy with you people. Also the name of a popular street dance, held every Wednesday night in Tivoli Gardens.

Pee pee.

To urinate. Usually used by the very young.

Peel head.

Refers to a bald headed person. "Yo, peel head bwoy."

Peeny wally.

A fire fly.

Peppa pot soup.

An extremely spicy hot soup made with callaloo, salted meat and peppers. It's very delicious.

Pickey pickey.

To be choosy.

Play play.

To make believe or pretend, such as when little children play house.

Play numba two.

To have anal sex.

Point yuh finga.

To accuse someone.

Pon di riva,
Pon di bank.

A dance move that originated in Jamaica. There was also a popular hit song by the same name.

Poppy show.

Someone who is always in the spotlight making an ass out of themselves.

Prem prem.

A pretty new marble.

Pretty pretty.
Extremely pretty.

Pum-pum.
Colourful term for vagina.

Pum-pum bush.
Pubic hair.

Puppa-lick.
A somersault. "Come mek we 'kin puppa-lick." Come, let us do somersaults.

Puppa Jesus!
Father Jesus! An exclamation.

Pussy 'ole.
The female anatomy, as well as a disrespectful term used to describe someone you don't like.

Pussy printa.
Very tight shorts or tights worn by women.

Pyaa pyaa.

Things of little or no consequence.

Quinge up.

To squeeze up or compress. Frequently heard on buses which are normally packed. "Nuh quinge mi up!"

Raise-up price.

A price increase. Always met with much displeasure by consumers.

Real Big Man

Used to describe someone who is wealthy and powerful or just someone who is well respected.

Rent-a-dread.

A male escort who is a Rastafarian or resembles a Rastafarian.

Ride de riddim.

When one's vocals is a perfect match for the beat.

Riggle mi dis, or riggle mi dat.

Riddle me this, riddle me that, guess me this riddle or perhaps not.

Rinch up yuh face.

To assume a very serious facial expression.

Ring an' line.

A marble game.

Riva wata.

Water from the river.

Rollin' calf.

A duppy (ghost) in the form of a cow that drags a chain and has fiery eyes.

Roll up a spliff. (illus.)

The act of rolling a marijuana joint. Yes, despite it's prevalence it is very much still illegal.

"roll up a spliff"

Roun' de caana.

Just around the bend.

Roun' table talk.

To gossip.

Row di boat.

Another new Jamaican dance move. This is done by imitating the rowing of a boat.

Ruff neck.

A local tough guy.

Run t'ings.

To manage or to be in charge. "A mi run t'ings!" I'm in charge!

Run-dung.

Mackerel, onions and peppers stewed down in coconut milk. A Jamaican staple.

Run off yuh mout'.

To persistently argue with someone.

Run de pussy red.

A man who is pleased with his sexual performance might brag that "He run de pussy red."

Scull school.

To play hooky.

Seh wha.

Say what. An exclamation.

Set guzzum.

To cast a spell on another.

Sheg roun'.

To bother someone. "Im a sheg roun' mi" He's bothering me.

Sheg-up. (illus.)

To mess up. "'Im jus' sheg up mi bisness!" He messed up my business.

"sheg-up"

Skin mi.

No, one is not requesting to be skinned alive, but is simply asking for a handshake.

Soon come.

Be there shortly. Don't hold your breath though, could be hours before they arrive.

Speakey-spokey.

When one travels abroad and on returning to Jamaica tries to speak with a foreign accent, he or she is said to be "Speakey-spokey".

Stamp an go.

A fritters made with salt fish, flour, salt, pepper and baking powder. Quite tasty.

Stay-home smaddy.

Refers to an individual who is un-employed or a housewife.

Stinkin' toe.

If someone offers you a "stinkin' toe", don't be offended, they're really offering you a type of fruit.

Shuga daddy.

A rich older man.

Su-su.

To gossip. "Dem a su-su pon yuh". They are gossiping about you.

Suck mi out.

An extremely disrespectful thing to say to someone. Most certainly will cost you a trip to the doctor.

Swallah mi spit.

To bite one's tongue. Maintaining your silence even though you want to make a comment.

Sweet nuh rass.

Very enjoyable. "Mi seh de food sweet nuh rass!" I really enjoyed the food.

Sweet sweet.

Very sweet.

Sweet up.

To attempt to charm someone or to get ready for a date.

Tan so back.

Don't participate, Just observe.

Teefin bwoy.

A boy who is a known thief.

Tear dung.

To create excitement and also to tell a female that you would like to "tear dung her wall", means you want to have sex with her.

Tek back chat.

To apologize. "Mi nuh tek back chat!" I don't make apologies.

Tek it stone dawg.

In abundance. "'Im 'ave so much money 'im can tek it stone dawg." He has a lot of money.

Tek set pon.

"Nuh badda tek set pon mi!" Don't constantly bother me.

Tek yuh out.

If someone threatens to "tek yuh out", they are planning to give you a one way ticket to the graveyard.

Two Year Old.

Term used to describe young teenage girls. Usually used by much older men who like to date these young girls.

Uptown girl. (illus.)

A female who is not from the ghetto but from the more affluent section of the city. (which is located uptown)

"Uptown girl"

Wagga wagga.

One who is fat and sloppy.

Walk 'bout.

Someone who is always seen everywhere is said to "walk 'bout".

Walk good.

In parting company you tell someone to "walk good". Goodbye, be careful.

Wanga gut.

A very greedy person.

War boat.

One who is always pushing for an altercation.

Wash belly.

The child that is born last is the "wash belly". Usually the mother's favourite.

Wash out.

To purge the body by taking a laxative.

Wata yuh garden.

Telling a female you want to "wata her garden", means you would like to have sex with her.

Watch yah now.

In anticipation of what is going to happen next. For instance a guy might be cheating on his girl and does not know that she's approaching, an observer might say "Watch yah now!"

Weh yuh deh?

Where are you?

What a clack a strike.

"Yuh nuh know what a clack a strike." You don't know what is happening.

Wheel an' come again.

To repeat or rewind. Usually heard at parties when the DJ is asked to play a song over.

White liva gal.

A girl who is sexually insatiable. Jamaican girls of Indian descent are reputed to have "white liva."

Willy bounce

A popular dance move that was created by the late dance hall icon, Bogle.

Wine up, wine up.

To move the lower torso in a sexually suggestive manner while dancing.

Wutliss bwoy. (illus.)

A young man who cannot sexually satisfy his girlfriend, is a "wutliss bwoy!"

"Wutliss bwoy"

47

Yuh dun know.

You already know. "Yuh dun know mi nuh like lazy people." You already know that I don't like lazy people.

Yuh face fava.

An expression used when cursing. "Yuh face fava fi hog." Your face looks like that of a hog.

Yuh mumma.

A rebuttal that you're advised not to use. Those are fighting words.

Yuh nuh know mi.

"You don't know what I'm capable of." Kind of like a warning.

Yuh nuh easy.

Used to express disbelief. Someone might tell you something outrageous they did and you respond "Yuh nuh easy".

"Zeen my yoot"

Yuh si di levels?

Do you understand what I'm saying?

Yuh si mi?

Do you understand me?

Yuh too hype!

Usually said to people who like to create excitement.

Zeen my yoot. (illus.)

A salutation used by young Jamaican men. Okay my friend.